LETTERS TO
SEABISCUIT

LETTERS TO
SEABISCUIT

SEVEN LOCKS PRESS

Santa Ana, California

Seven Locks Press
P.O. Box 25689
Santa Ana, CA 92799
(800) 354-5348

Individual Sales. This book is available through most bookstores or can be ordered directly from Seven Locks Press at the address above.

Quantity Sales. Special discounts are available on quantity purchases by corporations, associations, and others. For details, contact the "Special Sales Department" at the publisher's address above.

Printed in the United States of America

Library of Congress Cataloging-in-Publication Data
is available from the publisher
ISBN 1-931643-28-8

Cover and Interior Design by Sparrow Advertising & Design

In memory of Auntie Mar

TABLE OF CONTENTS

Foreword xi

Introduction xiii

October, 1938 through March 1, 1940 1

March 2, 1940 and Beyond 17

About Barbara Howard 117

"From the Paddock"

I was with Charles Howard when he bought Seabiscuit at Saratoga for $8,000, and I led him to the barn. He just walked along by himself. There was no lead pony, he didn't need one. Nothing ever bothered Seabiscuit. He was always that way, just an amazing, amazing, quiet, gentle, loving horse.

His jockey Red Pollard got hurt at Santa Anita and they didn't have anyone to work him. I was just a kid, eight or nine years old, and they had me gallop and breeze him with two other horses. Anybody could gallop Seabiscuit, anyone could breeze him. He was a big, gentle kitten, and he did everything just the way it was supposed to be done. A very, very intelligent horse.

Seabiscuit was a real competitor. He had that attitude that only the great ones have. He knew he could outrun any horse in the world. He would just be cruising along in a race, and he would flick one ear at the other horses just to let them know who was in control. Then if they challenged him, he would put both ears down, and the race was all over.

Seabiscuit was like rock star. He had great drawing power, and when he was scheduled to race more than 100,000 fans would show up at the track. He was truly a great, great racehorse.

Farrell "Wild Horse" Jones

Farrell Jones is one of the outstanding trainers in California history. He was the leading trainer at Santa Anita, Hollywood Park, Golden Gate Fields, and an unprecedented eleven consecutive years as leading trainer at Bing Crosby's Del Mar racetrack. Eighty years old, he now owns a rehabilitation center in Hemet, California, for more than 100 race horses.

The two greatest races of Seabiscuit's career were his victory over War Admiral in the Pimlico Special in the fall of 1939, and his fantastic comeback in the 1940 Santa Anita Handicap.

INTRODUCTION

"Commitment! There are only two creatures of value on the face of this earth: those with a commitment and those who require the commitment of others."
—*Abigail Adams, June 1776*

When you read this book of letters you will realize that it is a labor of love. This collection of letters focused on the love and devotion of an adoring public on one very special horse: Seabiscuit, or simply "The 'Biscuit" to his fans. This horse was many things to a past generation of Americans, but above all, he was an encouragement during tough times: the Great Depression and World War II. His is a story of teamwork, courage, endurance, strength, trust, and yes, commitment. This is crucial in understanding the "magic" of Seabiscuit both back when he lived, and even today.

Abigail Adams made the above statement to her husband, John Adams, to remind him of what he had once shared with her. She quoted it back to him during his period of greatest discouragement while away from home in Philadelphia, debating the question of American independence within the Continental Congress. Like most devoted wives, she had a real gift for encouragement.

I'm glad that I have this privilege to share a bit of the background behind this book because three very special women made it possible. Three remarkable women I have been blessed to know and consider close friends. I chose the above quote because like Abigail Adams, these three women were, and are incredibly gifted "encouragers" and women of commitment.

The first was my great grandmother Marcela Zabala Howard (I always knew her simply as "Auntie Mar"), devoted wife of Charles S. Howard ("Poppie"). She lived the entire epic of this wonderful horse and carefully saved and passed down this heritage to our family. She actually opened and read all of these letters first-hand as they began to arrive and continued throughout the career of "The 'Biscuit." For four decades, she lovingly saved them in a beautiful old wood treasure chest on a table behind her study desk.

My mother, Barbara Howard, is another incredible woman: "Mom" in its purest form, "Nanny" to my kids, best friend to my wife and me. Like a breath of fresh air from the Midwest, she married into the Howard family and endeared herself to Marcela. After decades of friendship, she was given these letters by "Auntie Mar" with the understanding that she would later know what best to do with them. This my mother has indeed done!

And lastly, to Laura Hillenbrand, an equally amazing woman and author of the blockbuster literary hit: *Seabiscuit, An American Legend*. Now also a "member for life" of our Howard Family (by informal adoption!), she set in motion the sequence of events which powerfully shared this amazing story to a new generation of Americans, and thus brought about the perfect climate for this work. Within Laura's latest, updated, fabulous edition, she shares a very special WWII story which has always meant a great deal to me, and now, having participated in the War in Iraq, takes on even new significance for this Marine.

In WWII, there were two known American bombers named "Seabiscuit", one a US Navy Lockheed PV-1 "Ventura" and the other a US Army Air Corps B-25 "Mitchell." Both crews were motivated to name and emblazon their aircraft after a horse (not some cheesecake portrait of a girl). To them, the 'Biscuit symbolized the spirit of a warrior: motivation, speed, endurance, and "true grit." Sadly, the entire Army crew was killed in action when their "Seabiscuit" took a direct hit during a courageous attack at low level upon a Japanese destroyer (other aircraft later bagged the enemy warship). It is this same strong, positive sense of patriotic

Our favorite photo of "Auntie Mar"

American spirit so well represented in the Seabiscuit legend that speaks encouragement to our nation and her faithful armed forces today. As Laura so accurately depicted, it is an American legend of confidence, determination, and dedication, one belonging to all of us as individuals and as a nation.

Finally, the story of Seabiscuit is a story of teamwork. The close-knit bond between my great grandfather, his horse, their trainer and jockey, is the very heart of Laura's masterpiece. Teamwork is also a strong American trait, for though we pride ourselves on our individualism, it is only through the former that truly great endeavors are accomplished. My great grandfather knew firsthand that with individual opportunity and ability, also went responsibility to others. He emphasized teamwork whether it was operating "team Seabiscuit" or running his Buick association. This same teamwork that got America through the Great Depression and made it supremely victorious in WWII is what today motivated a new generation of dedicated Americans fighting the war on terrorism in Afghanistan and Iraq. It is above all else an American legend of freedom, ability, hope, opportunity, encouragement, and commitment to others. It is simply what America is all about.

Letters to Seabiscuit is another part of this American legend. Thank you to Auntie Mar, Mom, and Laura for being committed encouragers in the way you have lived and live your lives!

I know you will enjoy *Letters* both for its historical context within this wide realm of current 'Biscuit fascination (epic book, TV specials, blockbuster film), and simply for the poignant expressions that this group of bygone Seabiscuit fans share with the America of today. There is much that we can learn from them about ourselves and our heritage.

Good reading. Good reflecting.

"Semper Fi," Mike Howard, Colonel, US Marines

The letters in this book are in their original form. Each received the personal attention of Marcela Howard. On several of the letters Marcela has written "sent picture." A photo of Seabiscuit was sent to these letter writers.

LETTERS 1939

TO

MARCH 1, 1940

I've speeded to the limit
Just because I want to say
Much love to you I'm bringing
From a friend who's far away

To
Sea Biscuit
The Darling of them all:
My Prayer is that you enter The
Santa Anita Handicap and show
your heels to them just as you did
to Star Admiral at Pimlico.
Oh! but that was grand.
Elizabeth Bachman,
Swedesboro, N.J.
One of your millions of admirers.

Dear Seabiscuit —
Lots of luck old
timer and keep the
"grass belly" down.
We're looking forward
to seeing a "Biscuit" Jr.
win the derby on fine
day —
Sincerely
Dobe & Oppy
Carey.

323 B. 67 Street,
Arverne, New York
October 25, 1939.

Dear Mr. Howard:-

How are you? It seems ages since I've heard from you. I hope this letter finds you "in the pink". The Special has me all keyed up and I'd like to let you know how I feel about it, so you can tell me how wrong I was after it's over. I'll never get over the shock that Kayak gave me when he left Cravat in the dust at Santa Anita.

To me Kayak is the handicap champion. He is quite capable of carrying his tremendous speed I 3/16. He has already bowed to Challedon at the Special distance, but he spotted the 3 yr. old 10 pounds, and had just come across the whole country. I favor "The South American Way".

Challedon is undoubtedly destined for immortality. Improving with every start, the Brann star had many experts who were willing to back him against Johnstown. He broke even with Big John in four starts. The 3 yr. old crown prince uses the Cunningham system of running when the top ones are slowing down. I wonder if you've noticed that he's been sticking much closer to the pace lately. Can it be that he's afraid Kayak will pile up too much of an early lead I don't think they'll pull the boner of going after Kayak the way they went after Johnstown in the Dwyer.

Isolater is stuck with the unenviable task of stepping out with Kayak. The Belair colorbearer is no speed-demon, but he's as game as they come and the distance is right down his alley.

Cravat has been licked by Kayak and Isolater. Although the Martin colt had some excuse in these defeats, it must be admitted that the distance is too short. At 2 miles we'd pick him to tow-rope this field but with 3 stars competing against him at their favorite distance we can't see him breaking in the money. If he makes his move with Challedon it will be a sight to see. They're the best stretch-running horses in the country.

Hash has been a mild sensation among the lesser lights, but each time he has encountered the biggies, he has tasted defeat. However, he always gives a good account of himself. The greentree star loves to come from behind.

In short, Mr. Howard, it seems to me that Kayak is getting a terrific break in that he has no speed horse to oppose him should he decide to step out and set the pace. If Johnstown were in the race I would pick Challedon to emerge the victor. He'll have to me a mighty fit horse to stave off Challedon's late rush, but then if he's picked up anything by being close to the Biscuit, he knows how to look 'em in the eye and make them yell "uncle".

Please let me know how The Biscuit is getting along. I see by the papers that he's coming along swell, and that you intend ~~brining~~ working him out at Tanforan. Do you intend giving him a prep race before the Anita or will you let his workouts suffice.? How about Kayak; will you pit him against the Biscuit in the big race? Boy, I wouldn't like to be in your shoes. I know whom your heart lies with. Nothing would please me more than to see The Biscuit displace Sun Beau, if only to show the critics how foolish they were in knocking him every time he dropped a nose decision to a plug that he spotted 15 pounds to.

Wishing you loads of luck and hoping to hear from you soon, I remain

Yours in sport,

Eddie Cohn

Box 142
Victorville, California
January 23, 1940.

Seabiscuit
In care of C. S. Howard,
Santa Anita Race Track
Arcadia.

Dear Biscuit;
    Don't let those legs of yours worry you another
day. I know there's the "devil to pay" after a workout, and
the old pins throb like an abcessed molar, so with that in mind,
winning the hundred grand must be farthest from your thoughts.
I have just what you need, in fact what every race horse needs
after a workout or race: to wit, the "Jake Boot", which contains
a highly curative clay. This boot I am talking about saved the
life of Joe Louis' (heavyweight champion, Joe) pet saddle horse
at Murray's Dude Ranch where Joe Louis trains on the Mojave
Dessert. His legs and hoofs were in such bad shape Joe was
ready to agree to have him destroyed. The "Jake Boot" was tried
as a last and almost hopeless effort to save him.
    Now then imagine this: his legs were so sore he flinched
when anyone gently touched them, and two of the hoofs were so
badly shrunken that they looked like hoofs of a Shetland Pony.
The very next day after the Jake Boots were put on, Joe's pet
had taken a new lease on life, and enjoyed his first meal in
months. In less than one month his hoofs were in condition to
be shod. What a grand and glorious feeling that must been, eh
Biscuit?
    Jake says that if you use these boots and clay as he
prescribes, and fail to regain your "sea legs" in time to win
the hundred grand, he will not charge your boss one thin dime.
But, as I said, Don't worry, the Jake Boot, and Silent Smith's
wise training, and your great heart will do all that thousands
ofhopeful fans are praying for --- Seabiscuit --- by 5 lengths.
    So be sure and tell Smith and Howard this boot that boots
home winners.

                Sincerely yours,

                J. F. Schmitt

P. S. I am a past master at horse shoeing, and though I have
retired from that strenuous work, I have not forgotten the many
winners I sent to the post, and what they needed to make them win.
The treatment prescribed by me positively does not contain
medicine, dope or stimulant of any kind what so ever.

        J. F. S.

Yale, Mich 2-21-'40

Mr. Chas. S. Howard
Dear sir: -
Being an ardent Booster for
Seabiscuit to surpass Sun Beau's record
earnings, I am herewith submitting my
findings in the field of animal nutri-
tion and research on physiological
reactions under maximum exertion.

The purpose of this plan of procedure is to bring about a closer approach
to circulatory & respiratory rhythmic
coordination which contributes to
metabolic equilibrium or as nearly so,
under maximum exertion, with a
decided tendency to forestall fatigue.

I might add that the sooner you can
put this plan into effect, the greater
the realization of your fondest hopes.

This plan is to be followed as closely
as conditions will permit in the actual
race, subject of course to your Trainer &
Jockey's judgement.

In the workouts directly following warm up gallop, have boy break horse into full speed for about 100 ft., then restrain to about a 25 sec. per quarter rating until reaching the stretch 3/16 pole, when restraint should be reduced slightly, at 1/8 pole reduce restraint entirely to finish line.

In the cooling out process, the drinking water is to be at a temperature of 85-90° fahr., to which add 4 oz. of fresh orange juice which gives an alkaline reaction and helps to reduce acids produced by catabolic action.

This procedure to be followed in each subsequent cooling out regardless of the amount of work performed, also increase the amount of orange juice by one ounce until you have reached 8 ounces, on the day of a race, if no exercise is given that morning, add only 4 oz. of orange juice to final drinking water which should be at about 55° fahr.

Wishing you the best of luck.

I am, very truly yours,

H. P. Smith

Yale + Detroit, Mich.

Los Angeles Calif.
Feb. 24, 1940

Mr. Charles Howard
Dear Sir: *Sent picture*

I take this liberty to
express my sentiments to
the greatest horse that ever
lived, your "Seabuscuit"
Mr Howard, I think you
are one of the most
fortunate men in the
world to own this great
horse, and to be able to
see him all the time.
I wonder if you
would send me a picture
of him suitable for
framing, I will be
listening and hoping

II

for him next Saturday
at my Radio, and when
its all over, I'll be as
happy as you, when
the announcer says
<u>Seabuscuit Wins</u>

Sincerly and
thank you

Henry Dochy
741½ Fetterly ave
Los angeles, Calif.

403 University Avenue
Oxford, Mississippi
February 25, 1940

Dear Mr. Howard,

 I hope you don't mind my writing you but as I like horses so well I thought maybe you would send me a picture of Seabiscuit and Kayak autographed by you.

 I'm fourteen years old and have always loved horses. I ride, have a scrapbook and many statues of horses. I talk about Seabiscuit so much that my school mates have nicknamed me "Biscuit".

 Seabiscuit has always been my favorite horse and I certainly was glad to open the paper this morning and see that Seabiscuit won the San Antonio handicap. I'm betting on 'Biscuit and Kayak to "do their stuff" next Saturday.

 Please, don't forget the picture. A snapshot will do.

    Yours truly,

    Patricia Penney
    403 University Ave.
    Oxford, Miss.

4636ª Page
St. Louis, Mo.
Feb. 26, 1940

Dear Mr. Howard,

In all possibility you may think this is a request from a nut, well maybe it is — but at that all nuts arn't cracked.

The favor I would like is this — will you send me the shoe from Seabiscuits most troublesome leg after the Santa Anita Handicap?

It may sound awful foolish but I think Seabiscuit is one of best horses for courage and stamina that ever lived.

Thanks a lot,

Howard Kyle

Saylesville, Rhode Island, February 27, '40.

Dear SEABISCUIT,
Santa Anita Track,
Arcadia, Cal.

I can't tell you how thrilled I was when I heard that you were training for your come back to the races. I wasn't down hearted when you did not win in those two sprints against fast horses. I knew you would soon find yourself and shine as of old.

Even if you had not won that race Saturday I would still have strung along with you. But when the news came that you had done so good I was more pleased than if some one had walked in and handed me a big roll of money. And, old boy, I want you to know that I am rooting, and hoping, and praying for your success in the big race. You can do it. And if the jockey on Kayak rides as he should, he can stave off interference and help both you and himself.

I wish Woolfe or Longden, or Meade were riding you though for I want you to win and that will place you on the pedestal for life as the world's greatest horse.

Tell your jockey to keep awake this time and not be afraid to look back coming down the stratch. It wasn't hard for Tod Sloan, Snapper Garrison, Fator, and others to do it to help their horses.

Never, in all history, was a great horse cheated out of three of the world's biggest purses by an INCH or less, as you were , because a jockey wasn't alert till he had passed the judges.

Biscuit, I have reached the proverbial three score years and ten. I have watched great horses come and go for sixty years. I have been with you since you were a baby. You have met all comers, at all distances, on all tracks, and never ran a bum race, and I will be with you as long as you are able to run.

And if bad luck should ever strike you and break your leg, ask Mr. Howard not to put you away. If you are near enough to me I will give my services free to put you in a sling and doctor your leg till it heals up again so that you can spend the rest of your days in a nice pasture and die a natural life. We used to have to doctor our cows broken legs when I was a kid and they got on the railroad track.

And, 'Biscuit, will you ask your boss to give me one of your racing plates when they are changed; also one from Kayak, and any of the other of your stable-mates that I have come to know so well. I will treasure them highly and keep them in my collection of souvenirs. My father was one of the early gold miners in Cal, and I have some of the things that he had in those days.

Good bye, old pal, watch your step, put everything into this big race and remember I will be on nerves all the time you are running , and wishing you the best luck that the gods can send you. YOU ARE GOING TO WIN. Keep telling yourself that and tell your jockey that he must feel the same way. This is your big day BUT, win or not, you can still make a world's record for yourself and your boss.

So long, *Thomas W. Snyder.*

TERMINIX INSULATION CORPORATION

1108 NO. CARROLL AT SWISS   •   TELEPHONE 8-1919   •   DALLAS, TEXAS

MBER OF WORLD'S LARGEST TERMITE CONTROL ORGANIZATION   •   LICENSED BY E. L. BRUCE CO., MEMPHIS, TEN

February 28, 1940.

Mr. C. S. Howard,
% Mr. Webb Everett, Racing Secretary,
Arcadia Park, California.

Dear Mr. Howard:

      The writer can not be in California
Saturday, to see the big race but my heart will be
with you, Tom Smith, Johnny Pollard and the grand
old warrior Seabiscuit.

      I am sure every red-blooded American,
who loves a fighter, wants to see the Biscuit carry
your colors to glory, in the "Tops of all Handicaps"
March 2nd. The old boy is entitled to win and I
sincerely hope he does.

      Down here, we have that grand song
" The Eyes of Texas Are Upon You " next Saturday,
the eyes of a whole nation will be on the " Ace of
the American Turf"

      When Seabiscuit answers the last
bugle call, which I hope will be some time yet, I
know of no finer epitaph than this.

        HE HAS FOUGHT A GOOD FIGHT,
          HE HAS FINISHED HIS COURSE,
          WE HAVE KEPT THE FAITH.

      Here is hoping for lots of sunshine
and an even break.

      Sincerely yours,

      Jim A. Davis

E. ZACHARIAH CROXALL
1131 SOUTH BURNSIDE AVENUE
LOS ANGELES, CALIFORNIA

February 29, 1940

Mr. C. S. Howard
Huntington Hotel
Pasadena, California

Dear Mr. Howard:

One of the most valuable possessions is that intangible thing we name fondness or - a better word - admiration. It is this intangible thing that has endeared Seabiscuit to not only all America but, I would say, to the world.

Some people may not be able to define it - they just seem to know it; others can say it in words. Animals, like human beings, have individuality, character and determination. They know what is about them and express their individuality in their own language. They also have appreciation for good treatment. That is why Seabiscuit is outstanding in his performances - that is why he is America's Sweetheart.

A successful race for Seabiscuit brings to him pride and satisfaction just as defeat brings disappointment, but success or defeat his spirit is always high and it is this attribute of your horse that commands respect from all peoples.

When you make a decision to scratch or go ahead, the love in your heart for Seabiscuit is the deciding factor. What if someone does object - you can always be assured that that someone does not understand.

So, Mr. Howard, what I have written is my contribution to America's greatest horse. Seabiscuit will go down in history as THE GREATEST.

All good wishes.

Sincerely yours,

Zachariah Croxall

EDWARD RAINEY
SAN FRANCISCO

2806 Vallejo St.,

Mr. Charles S. Howard,
San Francisco.

Dear Mr. Howard:

You have been very kind to send me photographs of Seabiscuit, with your Christmas good wishes. My thanks for both.

Somehow Seabiscuit has come to be more than just a great horse with a phenomenal record. He seems more like a personal friend. One feels like sending good wishes to him as well as to human friends. Who knows? Perhaps in that beautiful head of his he feels the affection so many people feel for him.

Again, thank you for your Christmas Greeting.

Sincerely,
Edward Rainey.

Dear Seabiscuit
I wouldn't bet a NICKEL

Dear Mr Howard
    You just can't imagin what a lot of pleasure and excitement you caused by sending me Seabiscuits picture. I was so thrilled. I shall always keep it. And I hope the great champion goes safely through his trial tomorrow and wins again. Thanks Again for your kindness. only a great man would have been so courteous.
        sincerely Sylvia Binford

MARCH 2, 1940

AND BEYOND

Charles and Marcela Howard

CHARLES F. HUTSLAR
MINISTER OF THE CLERGY
PASADENA, CALIFORNIA

March
2
1940   4:45 P. M.

The Howards:

Congratulations a thousand fold!

I suppose no other family in United
States, aside from your own, was more thrilled with joy at the magnificent triumph of
the BISCUIT than my own.

Two minutes after the race, our
daughter at Claremont phoned us long distance
expressing her exultant delight at his winning.
She said: " I am still shaking with feeling -
I was afraid the BISCUIT would lose."

Well, if you folk don't object, we
will purchase a Buick car and join the Howard
family, so we may acclaim a share in the world's
king of the turf - The SEABISCUIT.

I offered his picture to a man recent-
ly for $250.00 - but not now. He's worth a for-
tune to me after such a triumph.

Love and true friendly relations,

Charles F. Hutslar and
Family

19

37 Radcliffe Rd
Somerville
Massachusetts
March 1st 1940

Dear Mr Howard,—

No doubt you have received hundreds of congratulations from your many friends, please if you don't mind let me add mine.

I was so proud and happy, I watched the Biscuit from the time he was in Rockingham

You may have been the happiest man in the world when your horse won, but so was I, it was thrilling just to listen to the race on the Radio here in Boston, we here are really snow-bound, but I've seen Santa

Anita race track in it's beautiful
setting, so my memories carried
me back to California for the
running of that wonderful race

The radio is certainly a grand
invention for us working folks.

I do hope you'll bring
the Biscuit East this year

I was so disappointed the
day at Suffolks, As I had
the day off and a good seat,
but so it goes.

Congratulations to your trainer
Mr Smith and your jockey
Red Pollard you certainly have
a grand team.

Good - Luck

Best Wishes
Most sincerely
Mildred Holmes.

548 Veteran Avenue
W. Los Angeles

My dear Mr. Howard—
My hope
is that I can make this
coherent but just having
listened over the radio
to that blessed Seabiscuit,
not only win but break a
record I'm doubtful of it—
I've never seen him race
but never miss reading a
word that is written about
him, and have many pictures
of him in my scrapbook—I
love his gallant heart—
And Kayak II must also
have credit for his very

remarkable race, he is a fine fellow —

I know how happy you are at the outcome of this race, and so proud— Good luck to you Mr. Howard and please pat that beautiful "Biscuit" for me —

Most Sincerely
Irie Graves

(Mrs. G. M. Graves)

Mr. Charles H. Howard
Santa Anita Race Track
California

Please forward

General Delivery
San Carlos
California.
March 2nd - 1940

Dear Mr. Howard.

Have just listened to the "Seabiscuit" race over my radio, and I feel I *must* offer you my sincere congratulations. I am so very happy that dear little Seabiscuit proved to be such a good sport! I think the whole of the United States is happy for you — as I am! — I imagine todays race will go down in History as "The most Popular Win in America" — Probably in the world!

You may not remember me, but I had a pleasant hour with you and your family at Suffolk Downs, when Sahri II was beaten in the big Handicap!

I left Shockley eighteen months ago — I am now earning my *own* living, and incidentally very *much* happier!

With kindest regards to you, your very charming wife, and rest of family.

Very Sincerely
Eileen Shockley —

Royersford, Penna
Saturday March 2, 1940

My dear Mr Howard: —

I just heard the Santa Anita race — I cried for joy when my two favorites won. I love Seabiscuit as though he was my own — you are extremely lucky to own these two great thorough breds. And if I ever have the luck to see Seabiscuit, may I kiss him on his nose — Without joking. I have always wanted a lock of Seabiscuit's mane or tophair that would be part of him — I will be the happiest gal in the world if you

will send it to me — I do not believe there will ever be a thorough bred to equal him — I believe Mr Samuel Riddle is convinced of that to — So my best wishes to you Mr Howard and that wonderful little fellow Seabiscuit — Hoping you will grant my request I am yours

Gratefully and Sincerely
Laura Bell Johnson
Royersford
Penna.

3326 Cochran Ave
Los Angeles Calif.
March 1, 1940.

Dear Mr Howard,
You have two horses which my sister and I think are the best in the world. One is the champ Seabiscut the other is Lady Jacqueline. We think it would be a good idea, to mate them and call their fold Seajack. We call Seabiscut - Ocean-muffin for a nickname. We know the champ will do his best on Satur-day and win. I hope we will not take up to much of your time.
Yours Respectfuly
Jacqueline Age 9 and
Lorraine June Harris Age 10

Sun

My-my, folks, but it was wonderful to read this
morning of the Biscuit's triumphant gallop back
into the limelight. I'll bet you both had to have
your blood pressures looked into--right after the
race! I don't know anything that could do more for the
sport than to have a hero like Seabiscuit accomplish a
comeback. And his performance was a real tribute to
the training genius of Tom Smith; he's done a master-
ful job. Best reading of all was the report of the
big crowd's going wild as Biscuit moved into the lead.
Incidentally, Mrs Mac had his plate all polished up two
days ago! Somedday when you have one of his (just plain)
plates to spare, send it to George McManus ("Bringing Up
Father"), at Sunset Towers. He's a great pal of Earl
Anthony's, has a shoe of Man o' War's that I got for
him, and yesterday noon in Olsen & Johnson's (Hellzapoppin)
restaurant, he was telling that while he treasures the
Man o' War shoe, the one he'd like to have would belong to
a pet of his, Seabiscuit. He leaves for home tomorrow.
     Jock Whitney and Alfred are here for the legislative
doings that begin to morrow in Albany; they'll appear before
the committee considering a pari-mutuel enabling act, which
is expected to go through in March.
     Now here's wishing a 1-2 for you (with Lin and Bing
3d and 4th!) in the big race, and best of health to you both.
                    Sincerely,

                    Clemm Carchy

Chicago Ill.
3 - 3 - '40.

Mr. G. S. Howard,
Arcadia Cal.,

Dear Sir:

　　　If you are as good to Seabiscuit as
he has been to you, he will never again have to
look a starter in the eye.

　　　From this time on it should be for him
"THE LIFE OF RILEY".

　　　In sixty-five years of life, this is
the first time I have ever "butted" into another
man's business.

　　　　　　　Sincerely,

　　　　　　　James R Harris

　　　　　　　5451 Michigan Ave.
　　　　　　　Chicago, Illinois.

KMPC

★ ★ THE STATION OF THE STARS ★ ★

BEVERLY HILLS, CALIFORNIA

Sunday P.M.

G. A. RICHARDS
PRESIDENT

LEO FITZPATRICK
VICE-PRESIDENT

JOHN F. PATT
VICE-PRESIDENT

LEO B. TYSON
VICE-PRES. GEN. MGR.

BOARD
OF
DIRECTORS
★ ★ ★ ★
FREEMAN GOSDEN
"AMOS"
★
CHARLES CORRELL
"ANDY"
★
HAROLD LLOYD
★
BING CROSBY
★
PAUL WHITEMAN
★ ★ ★ ★

Dear Mr. Howard;

I Know I express the sentiment of Everyone at KMPC by extending my hearty congratulations for your spectacular win at Santa Anita yesterday.

More power to you and your Courageous champion Biscuit. You are both a great credit to the racing world.

Sincerely
G.A. Dick Richards

ASSOCIATE CBS STATION

"COVERS SOUTHERN CALIFORNIA LIKE THE SUNSHINE"

Chicago Ill
March 3rd 1940
Dearest Sea Biscuit.
Congratulations. you
ran a wonderfull race.
I have always liked you
I always said if you
could get a good trainer
you would go places. I never
cared much for Sun Beau, he
was a Bad Port actor, you
have always been a
gentleman. Biscuit I
always stuck with you
and I Know you Would
Win the anita Cap some
day. Please come to the
Chicago tracks this year
I am 4 9 years old and
a lover of good Horses.
I am very sincerely
Mrs Hattie Kish.
3239 West 54th St
Chicago Ill.

Chicago 3/8/40

Dear Charles.

It was a pleasant relief
for us to listen in to
the race broadcast at
6.30 PM our time, and we
were thrilled to hear
"Seabiscuit" come under
the wire winner.

A Great Victory which
the entire Country enjoyed.
The noise of the fans
almost drowned out
the Broadcast as the
Biscuit came in, and
one could nearly judge
the winner by the yells.
Cou heard your voice
to. Nodoubt hundreds of
Telegrams came in, cong
ratulating the Success.

We hope our letter reaches
you soon. Best wishes to all
from us. Sincerely Pearl & Herb

31

Dear Seabiscuit:

Kentuckians all over the world knew you could do it even before you showed the world. We knew it because:

The quitter gives an alibi,
The mongrel he gets blue,
The fighter goes down fighting,
But the thoroughbred comes through!

and you're a Thorobred.

Greetings to a Great Kentucky Horse from a humble Kentucky woman.

RBC

THIS SIDE OF CARD IS FOR ADDRESS

LOS ANGELES CALIF.
MAR 4
5 4 PM
1940

SEABISCUIT,
c/o Howard Stables,
Santa Anita Race Track,
Arcadia,
California.

Galt, Ontario,
'February, March 4 - 1940.

Dear Mr Howard,
I presume you are buried in messages of congratulation, but on behalf of my young daughter, husband and self, I do want to express the great thrill and joy we experienced when, as we sat breathless in front of our radio, we heard Seabiscuit proclaimed winner of the Santa Anita Handicap. I am sure you could not have been more anxious than we were, for that great moment. Really, I prayed all Saturday for his victory and promised to attend church more regularly, if my prayer was answered. Now, I feel it is up to me to do my part. And here's to your and his success in the Hollywood Gold Cup! It is always a heart break, that circumstances prevent us from attending these

these great races, so much enjoyed in days gone by. From childhood until the depression California was our winter home, and our daughter Marion was born in Hollywood — so it holds a dear spot in our heart. Again, with every good wish for your future success —

Very sincerely
"Seabiscuit's admirers"
Ida Simpson & family.

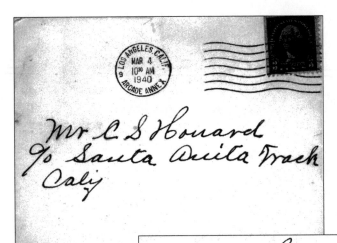

Mr C S Howard
% Santa Anita Track
Calif

Mr C S Howard –
Kind Sir,
I am a past 70
raised on a 700
a farm in Ken.
Where and where
great horses were
raised – Seabiscuit
has been a favor
-ite of mine since
his first line

light appearance -
I am writing this
to appeal to you
not to sell him so
he will finally end
up on a junk wagon,
he has made you
enough money that
you can afford him
a life of ease - and
if you cannot do
that shoot him out
right - instead a of
life of drugery
Please do not sell
him - I would so
much like to see him
but am unable to
do so - again
I plead with you
not to sell him
Respt
Mrs A P Asbury
919 Blaine St
L A

Gilbert Land Company

TIMBER, MINERAL AND FARMING LANDS

GRAND RAPIDS, MINN.   March 4, 1940.

Mr. Charles Howard,

Arcadia, California.

My dear Mr. Howard:

You do not know me from Adam, and
I have absolutely no business writing you about the horse,
but, with these preliminaries out of the way, may I ask you
to retire Seabiscuit while he is a fine able-bodied horse
so that he may enjoy a well-earned happy old age?

He had such a hard start, and has
done so well. I've never seen him in the flesh and don't
expect to but am always interested in his races, and lately
worried as well;   even if nothing happens to him, it
seems more fit that he end his racing career while he's up,
don't you think?

Whatever you decide, I wish him
happy days and many of them.

Very truly yours

Kathryn Gilbert.

On re-reading this, it sounds even more officious than I
thought. It might be better to ignore the lines, and read
between them.

RICHARD H. COLLINS
LOS ANGELES

March 4, 1940.

My dear Charlie:

At the end of the big race Saturday I wrote you a note
and sent it to your box by messenger but I doubt if it
reached you on account of the excitement.

During my life time, as you know, I have been fortunate in seeing some speed events especially in the old
days of automobile racing but I have never seen anything that had the effect on me that the victory of
Seabiscuit had.   Apparently I have been worrying
over him ever since he was hurt last year, but the
outcome of Saturday's race is the most gratifying
single event that has ever come to my attention.

Now listen: In the years gone by I frequently gave
you some advice and some times I have been inclined
to believe that you accepted it, and the suggestion
I am making herein is the end of the trail.   Let good
old Kayak carry the colors from now on and never permit Seabiscuit to see a race track again as long as he
lives.   He has done his stuff and done it well and why
not let him live his days as the greatest thoroughbred
that has ever lived.

Best regards and wishes to Mrs. Howard and yourself.

Sincerely yours,

RH Collins

Mr. C. S. Howard,
Huntington Hotel,
Pasadena, California.

LEON G. CAMPBELL, M. D.
MARVIN B. CORLETTE, M. D.
OAK KNOLL BANK BUILDING
COLORADO AT LAKE
PASADENA

March 4-1940-

Dear Mr. Howard :-

Watching Seabiscuit in his last two races, particularly last Saturday, was the biggest thrill I ever expect to experience in a sporting event. I am delighted for you.

I am only sorry Piggy could not have been here to see it.

I also resent the pseudo-experts who say Kayak should have won if he tried. What the hell does a horse have to do besides break the record and concede weight to be best?

Sincerely, Leon G. Campbell.

W. S. SEAMANS, JR.
PRESIDENT

SEAMANS LTD. - LOS ANGELES

REALTORS and BUILDERS
PHONE FITZROY 2191

RANCHES
BEAUTIFUL HOMES
COUNTRY ESTATES
BUSINESS INCOME
RESIDENTIAL INCOME
PROPERTY MANAGEMENT

3505 WEST SIXTH ST.
JUST NORTH OF
"COCOANUT GROVE"
"BROWN DERBY HAT"
"CHAPMAN PARK PUEBLOS"

March 4th, 1940.

PERSONAL

Dear Mr. Howard:

Well after such a wonderful
Saturday afternoon and the Gold Cup Saturday
night or Sunday morning, you should be feeling
about "tops" - which you are.

No real person who knows you
begrudges one iota of your joy and success, for
they do know you are a 100% true sportsman with a
backbone instead of only a wishbone.

As Louella Parsons is forever
saying "Don't say I didn't tell you" - remember
my telegram to you at Pimlico last November 1st,
after the Kayak II - Challedon race when I said

"Sorry but we know you never quit so hurry back
home and get Seabiscuit ready for the Santa Anita
handicap".

With kindest personal regards

Very sincerely,

W. S. Seamans, Jr.,
President

To:
Mr. Charles S. Howard
Huntington Hotel
Tanner House
Pasadena, California

WSS:PJB

SPECIAL DELIVERY
BUSINESS AND RESIDENTIAL RENTALS

HARRY ELLIOTT
MONADNOCK BUILDING
681 MARKET STREET
SAN FRANCISCO

March 4, 1940

Dear C. S.:

We were all so happy over Seabiscuit's victory and just wanted to tell you
so.

Yesterday at the meeting of the
Promotion and Publicity Committee of the Golden
Gate International Exposition for 1940, I sug-
gested that the Fair name a day for Seabiscuit
as a tribute to C. S. Howard, San Franciscan,
and Seabiscuit, San Francisco thoroughbred and
the world's greatest.

I believe that this would be the
first time that any Exposition has so honored
a horse and it would be a tribute well deserved
by both the horse and its owner.

Cordially yours,

Harry Elliott

HCE:lh

WILLIS SHARPE KILMER
REALTY AND THOROUGHBRED DEPARTMENT
BINGHAMTON, N. Y.

March 4,1940.

Mr. and Mrs. Charles S.Howard,
   1601 Van Ness Ave.,
     San Francisco, California.

Dear Mr. and Mrs.Howard:

        You have reason to be very proud
of your splendid Seabiscuit. He is a gallant, courageous
horse and truly a champion. Our own great Sun Beau, in
relinquishing his crown to Seabiscuit, is assured of an
eminently worthy successor.

        But to us it seems that to you,
and to Mr. Smith, who have been so patient when injury
threatened to deprive you of the prize and who have brought
back your horse with such consummate skill, no small meed
of credit and praise is due. Your handling of your valiant
champion should be an inspiration to those who are too
readily prone to concede defeat.

        Mr. Kilmer has not been well, but
he joins me in extending to you and to Mr. Smith sincerest
congratulations and best wishes.

                Cordially,

             Jane Wells Kilmer

Mrs.W.S.K./C.L.E.

41

Church of the Holy Angels,
1104 So. Baldwin Ave.,
Arcadia. Calf.
March, 4th, 1940.

Dear Mrs Howard,

may I express to Mrs.
Howard and self my congratulations and
felicitations on the victory of
Seabiscuit and, of course, of

Kayak, II.

The victory, no doubt, was
most pleasing, but, I am
sure, its popularity was
equally sweet and acceptable.

Assuring you of my joy
in your victory, and with
sincere best wishes,

I remain,
Respectfully Yours,
(Fr.) Gerald M. O'Keeffe.

Box 504,
Arcadia. Calf.

Mrs Charles S. Howard,
c/o Santa Anita Race Track,
Arcadia. Calf.

FAIR ACRES
WESTTOWN, PA.

**SADDLE HORSES
AND
HUNTERS**

BREEDERS OF

THOROUGHBRED HORSES

AND

REGISTERED JERSEY CATTLE

**VIRGINIA
"Red"
FOX HOUNDS**

H. G. and C. L. TWADDELL
OWNERS

WESTTOWN 2124

Mar.4-1940

Mr.Charles S.Howard
San Francisco
Cal,

Mr.Charles S.Howard
Dear Sir:

I will ask you to pardon the liberty I am taking in writing to you.

But, I cannot help extending my congtatulations to you on the victory of the great Seabiscuit in the Santa Anita Handicap.

I recieved the greatest thrill of my life as the report of the race
came over the air.

I have been interested in every move this great thoroughbred has
made,there is no doubt in my mind that Seabuscuit is the peer of
any thoroughbred the world has produced.

I saw him when a two year old,in the stable of my old friend,James
Fitzsimmons and have followed his racing career with great interest,
almost praying that he would achieve his goal as the greatest money
winner of the world.

Today, I congratulate you,Sir, in the faith you have had in this
outstanding horse.

I have perhaps, a personal interest as a breeder of thoroughbreds
in a modest way.

I am enclosing the pedigree of a yearling filly,which promises to
develope into a filly of much class,you will note how closely she
follows the bloodlines of your great horse.

May I add, that I hope Seabiscuit will prove himself an outstanding
sire.

      Long may he live.

        Very resp.yours.

          Horace G. Twaddell

A. B. HANCOCK
PARIS, KY.

March 4th, 1940

C. S. Howard, Esq.,
1601 Van Ness Ave.,
San Francisco, California.

Dear Mr. Howard:

     It was a great pleasure to all of us here
to see SEABISCUIT come back and put up such a splendid race
on Saturday. Please accept my heartiest congratulations and
also extend them to Mr. Smith on the wonderful job.

     With best wishes,

     Sincerely yours,

6911 Clinton St., L. A.
Monday, March 4th, 1940.

Dear Mr. Howard:

Have written you about our dearly be-
loved Seabiscuit before.

And suppose I shouldn't take the
time nor the effort to write again, when, no
doubt, you will think I should attend to my own
business.

Mr. Howard, PLEASE, retire Seabiscuit
to green pastures and a life of ease. And hasn't
he earned it? He has brought you fame and glory
and reached the goal you had for him and why ask more?

He is getting older every day and
I couldn't even watch the race the other day for fear
with his big heart and sticktoitivness that he might
stumble and break one of his legs and have to be
destroyed.

You have such a great horse like
Kayak to run in the Hollywood Gold Cup for you so
why risk the Life of Seabiscuit any further.

I know you think too much of him to
take any further chances with him.

Please, Mr. Howard, take care of
him while you have the chance and before it might be
too late.

Respectfully,

Mrs. W<u>m</u> B. Simpson

PS This is not one of those crank letters.

O. W. HUFF
PRESIDENT

CESAR SOTO
VICE-PRESIDENT

L. JUDD
SECRETARY

BUSINESS MEN OF SAN YSIDRO

SAN YSIDRO, CALIFORNIA

March 4 1940

C. S. Howard
Arcadia Calif.

Dear Sir,-

     The Business Men of
San Ysidro want to congratulate you
on SEA BISCUIT'S winning Saturday.

     Yours Very Truly,

Secretary

Judd

"Poppie" on Chulo and Auntie Mar on Seabiscuit and scotty, Wee Biscuit, at Ridgewood Ranch

ERNEST SCOTT

J. HOLLAND SCOTT

Hampshirdown Sheep
Hampshire Hogs

Ringlet Barred Rock Chickens

Shipping Point:
BIRDS NEST, VA.

Chatham Farm

SCOTT BROS.

Bridgetown, Virginia

Mar, 4th 1940

Mr. C. S. Howard
Los Angeles,
Cali:

Dear Sir:
Congratulations to you,
and hats off to Seabicuit
with kindest regards to Kayak II.

Yours very truly
Ernest Scott

Lover of a good horse

March 4, 1940

Mr. C. S. Howard,
    Arcadia, Cal.
My dear Mr. Howard,
                Congratulations!
I'm glad Sea Biscuit (God bless
him) won the big race But.
    I have never even seen you-
Mr. Smith nor Pollard, but I
did see Sea Biscuit put
War Admiral away—and the
way he did it gave me the
greatest thrill I ever had on
the track — I hadn't a penny
on that race — nor this one —
and my only interest is love
for a wonderful horse and
admiration for the men who
had enough faith and patience
to work with him. Sea Biscuit
and I have something in
common — rheumatism — so I
do understand.
    Please give him an extra pat
for me, and may god luck
be yours.
            Yours very truly,
            Mrs. A. B. Cross
            1278 Park Ave.,
                Plainfield, N.J.

WALLACE FRANCIS HAMILTON
21XXIXXXX XXXXXXXXXXXXXXa
SAN DIEGO, CALIFORNIA

STUDIO EIGHT
Spanish Village Art Center
Balboa Park
March 4th.,
1 9 4 0

Mr Charles S. Howard
Santa Anita Track
Arcadia, California

Dear Mr. Howard:

No doubt a thousand hungry or
otherwise artists have importuned you to paint
the great SEA BISCUIT-- so here is offer number
one thousand and one!

Are you the Howard I knew in
San Francisco, I wonder -- in a business way,
I mean? When not drawing pictures along the
embarcadero I sold magnetos for the Remy Electric
Company. But probably I am mistaken.

I have sold paintings of race
horses and horses racing to Jim Coffroth and
others down through the years. I have spent
many interesting years learning to draw horses --
at the old Tijuana track, on the art staff of the
San Diego Union and six years in the United States
Cavalry.

What a horse! And how he makes my
painting fingers tingle. I have a way of getting action
and drama into horse painting that might interest you.
I should like to preserve on canvas for an admiring
posterity the most remarkable SEA BUSCUIT.

May I extend an invitation to you and
to Mrs Howard xxxxixxxitatixx to visit mys studio when
in San Diego?

Cordially,

Wallace F Hamilton

Old Hickory Farm
Inc.
Phil T. Chinn, President
Lexington, Ky.

March 4, 1940.

Address all Communications to
Office in Hernando Building

Farms { Maysville Pike
         Johnston Pike

Mr. C. S. Howard,

1601 Vanness Avenue,

San Francisco, California.

Dear Mr. Howard:

      First of all, SEA BISCUIT's victory was
very popular in Kentucky because of the fact that he was bred
and reared here. I think Tom Smith has demonstrated beyond
a peradventure of doubt that he is one of the stand-out horsemen
of this century. The public does not know SEA BISCUIT as I do,
and I think in view of his ailments, for him to have won this great
race and beaten the best horses for the past years, is a real
accomplishment. I hope he carries on and wins a few more classics
before being retired to the stud and that when he is retired, he
will have some colts that will carry on in like manner.

      Please give Tom Smith my regards.

      Sincerely yours,

Phil T. Chinn

Sea Biscuit.

A man and his horse had been trying so long
The rainbow to reach, – but thing always went wrong;
So near, yet so far from, their goal had they dwelt,
The torture of heart-wrenching failure they'd felt.

Came the day when the last chance of reaching their goal
Was upon them and each knew within his own soul,
This day they'd not fail – Sun Beau's record they'd beat
With the heart of a champion and his fast flying feet.

The sound of the cheers of the thousands who came
This race of the century to witness were tame
Compared with the pounding within one man's breast, –
The man whose brave horse was to face his great test.

"He _must_ win to-day", his mind said, and his heart
Echoed "must" and then "Will" just before the big start;
"They're off!" came the words and thirteen thoroughbreds ran
As one from the start as but real champions can.

Around the first turn with Seabiscuit fifth place;
His jockey alert, – "We will win" on his face;
To second place next, at the turn, he was brought
And kept there until the stretch battle was fought.

And then they were off, really off, down that track,
As horse and frail jockey made one grand come-back;
The cheers upon cheers were as nectar to one
Who the rainbow had reached when his Seabiscuit won

Sylvia Sharp.
1940

Mr. C. S. Howard,
% Santa Anita Race Track,
Arcadia,
California.

Personal

TAOS AUTO COURT
Capt. Irving O'Hay

March 5, 1940

TAOS, NEW MEXICO

My dear Mr Howard,

We too wish to extend our congratulations for the amazing victory and the grand comeback of the Champion.

You deserve such success, as you have proven to be a fine sportsman by sticking to Red Pollard who used excellent judgment, and your even better judgment in employing such a master conditioner as Tom Smith. All three of you have given the Champion—Seabiscuit—so much of yourselves that he, with good horse sense gave it back to you.

More power to you—

TAOS AUTO COURT
Capt. Irving O'Hay

TAOS, NEW MEXICO

I am writing this, while Capt
is vastly improved he still
Cannot write. And it is his
illness that prevented us from
being there to witness Seabiscuit
Victory and your joy.
However if luck smiles we
will see you next year.
Regards from us both
Sincerely
Dorothy O'Day.

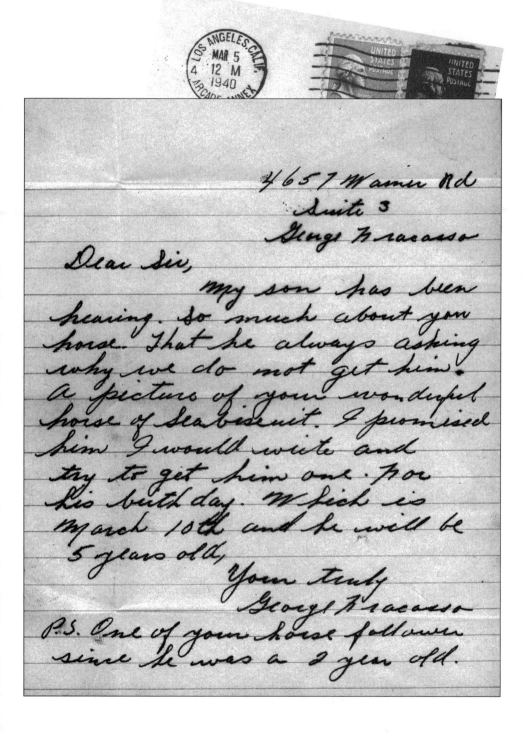

4657 Warner Rd
Suite 3
George Niracasso

Dear Sir,

my son has been
hearing. so much about your
horse. That he always asking
why we do not get him.
a picture of your wonderful
horse of Seabiscuit. I promised
him I would write and
try to get him one. For
his birth day. Which is
March 10th and he will be
5 years old,

Your truly
George Niracasso

P.S. One of your horse follower
since he was a 2 year old.

Tel. GRamercy 5-4863-4864

ON SALE AT ALL NEWSSTANDS

Published Every Day Except Sundays
by New York Daily Tab, Inc.

Representatives
At All Tracks
Throughout
the Country

The
Fearless
Independent
Racing Daily

DAILY RACING

7 WEST 22nd STREET

NEW YORK CITY

March 5, 1940

Mr. & Mrs. C. S. Howard
1601 Van Ness Avenue
San Francisco, Calif.

Dear Mr. & Mrs. Howard:

I want to take this opportunity to congratulate you both on your splendid victory in the
Santa Anita. Seabiscuit and Kayak II will go
down in the history of horsedom as the greatest
horses that ever circled the oval.

I am glad from another point of view that your
horses won because I know how sincerely devoted
you both are to the steeds and that your
interest in winning this race is purely from
the sportsmanship angle and not so much from
the monetary standpoint.

However, the happiness derived from it should
stay with you throughout life. Please believe me when I say that I am gratified and
wish you continued success in racing. You're
a great combination: Mrs. Howard, Mr. Howard,
Mr. Smith, Seabiscuit and Kayak II.

Good luck to you and continued success.

Sincerely yours,

DAILY RACING TAB.

Publisher:

TE:RB

61 Woodlawn Avenue West
Toronto 5, Ontario

March 5th 1940

C. S. Howard, Esq.,
1601 Van Ness Avenue,
San Francisco, Cal.

Dear Mr. Howard:

You must be one of the happiest men
in the land. Many of the rest of us are very happy
too along with you, as Seabiscuit is our favourite
horse, and we follow him all over the map. For myself
I like Seabiscuit best because he has so many fine
characteristics, and there is so much romance in the
story of his life.

There is, no doubt, a good deal of
truth in what the newspaper writers say about the
popularity of Seabiscuit being due in a large measure
to his appearing all over the country, thus giving
many people the thrill of seeing him.

There is only one thing money buys that
I envy. It is the power it gives you to indulge your
love of horses.

Your victory comes at such a fine time,
too, as so many of us saw the short MOVIE OF THE LIFE
OF SEABISCUIT.

Congratulations to you and Mrs. Howard!

Yours sincerely,

(Miss) Flora Mackenzie

FMM

MORNING   EVENING   SUNDAY

THE SUN

THE A.S. ABELL COMPANY, PUBLISHERS
BALTIMORE, MD.

March 5,1940

Dear Mr.Howard:

       Thought maybe you were keeping a scrap book on Seabiscuit and these might be added to the collection.

       If not,thought possibly you and Mrs.Howard would like to see how handsomely Seabiscuit wears his crown.

       All joking aside,we in Maryland were almost as thrilled as you must have been and we're happy for your sakes.

       Hope you continue to have good fortune with both the 'Biscuit and Kayak II and that we'll have the pleasure of seeing you soon at Pimlico. Mrs.Reed joins me in sending best regards.

       Yours truly

       Don Reed

L. L. DAVIS, D. D. S.
MEDICO-DENTAL BUILDING
2111 EIGHTEENTH STREET
BAKERSFIELD, CALIF.

March 5, 1940

Mr. C. S. Howard
Santa Anita Race Track
Arcadia, California

Dear Sir;

      Enclosed is a check for one dollar. Would you please be kind enough to send me a nice picture of Seabiscuit about 10" x 8" suitable for framing, as I want very much to have his picture in my den.

      If this check is not sufficient to cover the cost of the picture and the mailing charges, please let me know and I'll gladly send you whatever it casts.

      His race last Saturday was about the biggest sports event in years. Trusting that the old warrior lives to be at least thirty,

                Sincerely

                L. L. Davis

                L. L. Davis D.D.S.

LLD/AG

P. S. Any size, 10" x 8" or over is O. K.

Sent picture

60 EAST 42ND STREET
NEW YORK, N.Y.

March 5, 1940.

Dear Marcella and Charlie:

Thanks for your wire. I did not wire you after the race as you probably received hundreds of wires, so I thought I would wait a day or two and write you, and want to take this opportunity to send our heartiest congratulations.

It was really a marvelous performance; it only shows what patience and perseverance will do, and how good sportsmanship will be rewarded. I don't suppose you have really come down to earth yet - I don't see how you could after such a performance. In addition to what the Biscuit did, it is a wonderful thing to have two horses in the same stable who could run 1 - 2 in such a race.

I don't suppose you have made up your mind whether you will retire him or not, but if he came out of the race well and sound, there is no reason why he should not go on and run it over the $500,000 mark and really give them something to shoot at that will probably never be equalled during our generation, anyway. You know how we feel and there isn't much more I can say, only that we were delighted.

I am enclosing a clipping from yesterday's Sun which I think is rather amusing, and you may not see it.

Looking forward to seeing you both when you get back here this Spring, and with best wishes for continued success, I am,

Sincerely yours,

Earle

Mr. & Mrs. Charles Howard,
Howard Automobile Company,
California and Van Ness Avenue,
San Francisco, California.

To The Biscuit

Must thou try again, Seabiscuit?
Must thou bear the heavy weight?
That the handicapper has assigned thee,
America's tribute to her great?

To gain the greatest glory,
That g wearing Sun Beau's crown,
Must thou bear the heavy burden
That broke Discovery down?

In '37 Anita's Handicap,
Thou had'st within thy clasp,
When, "I knew not Rosemont was so close"
Poor Pollard, was heard to gasp.

And once again, thou would'st have been
The leader on Fame's scroll,
But weighted down with telling pounds
Light-weight Stagehand, took thy toll.

In Nov. on old Hill-top,
When they staged a special race.
There soon should'st thou Imperial Uncle
That he could'nt stand the pace.

And then again in '39.
Santa Anita's Barrier, thou would'st have faced
But an accident befell thee,
And Kayak II. took thy place.

And should'st thou this time be defeated.
All who love thee well. shall know,
Twas not for lack. of speed. or Courage.
But the handicapper's blow.

But Oh! should'st thou, win Seabiscuit
How glad a world will be.
That thou hast won. thy well earned glory
And art. safe for Posterity.

THE KANSAS CITY STAR.

DAILY	SUNDAY	WEEKLY
COMBINED CIRCULATION MORNING AND EVENING 600,000	CIRCULATION 320,000	CIRCULATION 450,000 PAID-IN-ADVANCE SUBSCRIBERS

Wednesday, March 6, 1940.

Charles S. Howard

San Francisco,

Dear Mr. Howard:

     To settle an argument among two supposedly turf experts will you please tell me just exactly what purchase price you paid Odgen Mills for Seabiscuit at Saratoga in 1936.

     As a writer of newspaper articles and a writer for the Turf And Sport Digest I would like to know this.

     Thanking you now for the information, I am

Most Respectfully

Robert K. Kelley

Robert K. Kelley

Kansas City Star

18th and Grand

Kansas City, Missouri

Charles Howard paid $8,000 for Seabiscuit, between August of 1936 and March of 1940, Seabiscuit's earnings were $437,730.

SOUTHERN PACIFIC LINES

SOUTHERN PACIFIC COMPANY
SOUTHERN PACIFIC RAILROAD COMPANY OF MEXICO
TEXAS AND NEW ORLEANS RAILROAD COMPANY
SOUTHERN PACIFIC STEAMSHIP LINES

"MORGAN LINE"

HUGH H. GRAY,
GENERAL PASSENGER AGENT

W. F. COYNE,
TRAVELING PASSENGER AGENT

PASSENGER TRAFFIC DEPARTMENT
535 FIFTH AVENUE

IN REPLY PLEASE REFER TO
FILE: 4715

NEW YORK, N. Y.,

March 6 1940.

Mr. Charles S. Howard,
1601 Van Ness Avenue,
San Francisco, Calif.

Dear Mr. Howard:

It was a thrill to hear your voice over the radio on Saturday saying "it is something we have been trying four years to do".

Knowing your affectionate regards for Seabiscuit, think I can appreciate the great joy that must have come to Mrs. Howard, Tom Smith and yourself in seeing America's Favorite Horse come through in such splen did fashion.

It would appear that Seabiscuit must have realized there was a question in the minds of some as to whether any horse (even a Seabiscuit) would accomplish what he was aiming to do. There was only one thing left to do and that was to make it convincing. The new track record was his response.

We, who have grown to love Seabiscuit, rejoice with you in his brilliant victory, and look forward to seeing him, as well as Kayak II during the coming Summer Meetings back East.

Sincerely yours,

W. F. Coyne

THE WEST'S GREATEST TRANSPORTATION SYSTEM
ALL TRAINS ON SOUTHERN PACIFIC'S FOUR SCENIC ROUTES ARE COMPLETELY AIR-CONDITIONED

March 6 1940

Dear Mr. Howard

I am a boy 14 years old weight 90 lbs and I hope to be a jockey some day. I am very much interested in Horses. From different articles in the paper it looks like you are going to retire Seabiscuit. They say Challedon is a good horse, he beat Kayak II but that doesn't make much difference because Seabiscuit beat Kayak II and in excellent time. This time has never been equaled by Challedon and I think Challedon is just another War Admiral. The horses of the east don't seem to equal the horses of the west. I am a sound follower of Seabiscuit and I am rooting for him all the time he's racing. According to the time Seabiscuit made in the Hundred Grander, he is in the best condition he has ever been in and is ready for a match race with Challedon. The match race would be held in Pimlico worth fifty thousand dollars. I know the money doesn't make much difference but the glory of Seabiscuit means a lot. With jockey Johnny (Red) Pollard in the boot Seabiscuit is hard to beat. Don't break Seabiscuit's spirit by retiring him.

Sincerly
Claude McCabe
3202 Walnut
Street Huntington Park
California

65

Portland Dec. 3.6.41.

Dear Mr Howard-
I received the picture of
Seabiscuit you mailed me OK, and I do
most sincerely thank you. I will get a
nice frame for it today.

Moiland made a most
wonderful showing last Saturday in the
big race. I heard it here in Portland by
radio. He is yet a young horse. I hate to
see them imposing 130# on him in a mi
+ 1/2 this coming Saturday. I have always
said they have handicapped Howard
horses too much and made it just as
hard as possible for them to win. If I
ever see charlie Strubes, I surely intend
to tell him so too, in no uncertain way.
Seabiscuit was always overloaded, and if
the poor fellow had its hour been, he would
have won two more of their other big ones.
With every good wish Mr Howard
I am, Sincerely yours,
Harry L. Porter

% Gen. Del.

Dear Mr. Howard :—

Congratulations! What a thrill! Caught the broadcast over the radio & could just picture "old gallant-heart" pounding down the stretch.

You & Tom Smith deserve all the credit in the world for a remarkable exhibition of skill & patience. I can't explain the silence of the Eastern papers except that The Biscuit has amazed them so often that nothing he can do from now on will faze them. What do you intend doing with the Biscuit now? It seems a shame to retire him if he came out sound. Of course, the greatest thing you could do would be to match him with Challedon, if you feel he could stand another training grind. The Eastern Seaboard is all for Challedon & the biggest race this season will probably be a match between Bimelech & the Brann colt.

Hoping you're enjoying good health

Eddie

Eddie
323 B. 67 ST.
Brooklyn, N.Y.

ROCKAWAY N.Y.
MAR 2
7-PM
1940

THIS SIDE OF CARD IS FOR ADDRESS

Mr. Charles S. Howard
1601 Van Ness Avenue
San Fransisco, Calif.

PLAN TO VISIT NEW YORK WORLD'S FAIR

The VANDERBILT Hotel
Park Avenue at Thirty Fourth Street
New York

March 7, 1940

Mr Charles S. Howard
Sanfrancisco, California
Dear Mr Howard;

Last year I was in California
And used to watch, as well as "bet"
on Seabiscuit. The last day I
didn't mind my losing my bet at
Santa Anita when he ran in the
big race, but coming so near, was
too bad. I felt Seabiscuit felt it too.
knew he'd lost, and was kind of
heart sick as human beings are.
That he won this year makes us
who knew Seabiscuit, rejoice with
his being so courageous

I am writing some short fiction
stories. I want to include Seabiscuit.
Will you tell me some interesting
things about him.
Sincerely Yours
Bess Skinner

THOMAS & THOMAS
ATTORNEYS-AT-LAW
UKIAH, CALIFORNIA
TELEPHONE 412

March 7, 1940.

Mr. Chas. S. Howard,
1601 Van Ness Ave.,
San Francisco, California.

Dear Mr. Howard:

As you have now probably had time
to read all of the telegrams and letters received,
congratulating you on the unprecedented victory of
your great Seabiscuit at Santa Anita on last Saturday,
I send mine. Before the race, I confess I did have
considerable anxiety about the result for fear that
his former trouble might reappear and rob him of his well
earned and rightful laurels, and when my son who was
listening to the radio in another room came in and said
"Seabiscuit won, Kayak second", I cannot find words to
adequately express my delight. Now that the ordeal is
over and the great horse has established himself as the
Super Horse in all American turf history, I can rest.
Seabiscuit is not only a great horse. He
is more, a great benefactor. I have no doubt that his
victory has brought more real joy to more California
hearts than any other event that has transpired this year,
and that is a genuine benefaction.
Whatever may come to him in the future,
owing to his advancing years, his record and his fame
are established beyond the reach of detraction or
question. He is numbered now among the Immortals.

Yours truly,

W. P. Thomas

WPT:H

MEMBERS: AMERICAN BANTAM ASSOCIATION : CALIFORNIA RARE AND FANCY FOWL CLUB : SAN GABRIEL VALLEY POULTRY ASS'N.

BREEDING STOCK   BABY CHICKS   HATCHING EGGS

REG. W. JONES
Specializing in
S. C. WHITE LEGHORN
BANTAMS

"THE JONESES"
321 North Bartlett Street
San Gabriel, California

ETHEL S. JONES
Breeder and Exhibitor
S. C. ENGLISH WHITE LEGHORNS
(TOM BARRON STRAIN)

March 9th.
1 9 4 0.

Mr. Charles. S. Howard.,
1601 Van Ness Avenue.
San Francisco. California.

Dear Mr Howard:

      I have again been appointed Superintendant of
Bantams for the 1940 Poultry Show to be held at Santa Anita
Race Track, at approximately the dates of last year (Nov 28th
to Dec 3rd)

      To perpetuate the achievement of champion
"SEA BISCUIT" at this Track in this year I would like to ask
you if you would donate a Trophy or Plaque suitably inscribed
to the Champion Bantam of the Show and to be known as the
"Sea Biscuit" challenge trophy, such trophy or plaque to be
won THREE consecutive years before becoming the absolute
property of the exhibitor.

      Anticipating a Show that will surpass last
year, I am working hard to secure a record breaking entry list
on my end of the programme (Bantams) and if promises materialise
into entries I shall be well repaid for my efforts.

      I would be pleased to hear from you.

Yours very truly.

Reg. W. Jones

P.S. I would like to see the birds you purchased last year
    entered at this Show.

'Phone

2255 Cheremoya ave.
Hollywood Calif Mar 4-40

Mr C. S. Howard
Los Angeles Calif.

Dear Mr Howard:-

According to the papers you
promised Seabiscuit retirement,
if he would win the Santa Anita
One hundred thousand dollar
handicap for you. That
promise mean't much to those
of us who love him.

He won gloriously, he has
striven nobly in all of his
efforts. Now we read that he
may continue on as long
as he is in good condition
Give him a break.

Why wait until he again cripples himself or bursts his gallant heart in his effort to win for you?

Be as sporting as he is courageous and let him have his reward while he is able to enjoy it. This, rather than forced retirement because of injury or breakdown.

I am not a horsewoman or a race track follower. I do however, love Seabiscuit, and am one of his most sentimental fans.

May he live long and be happy in his years of rest. Just a fan

(Mrs) A. B. Magie

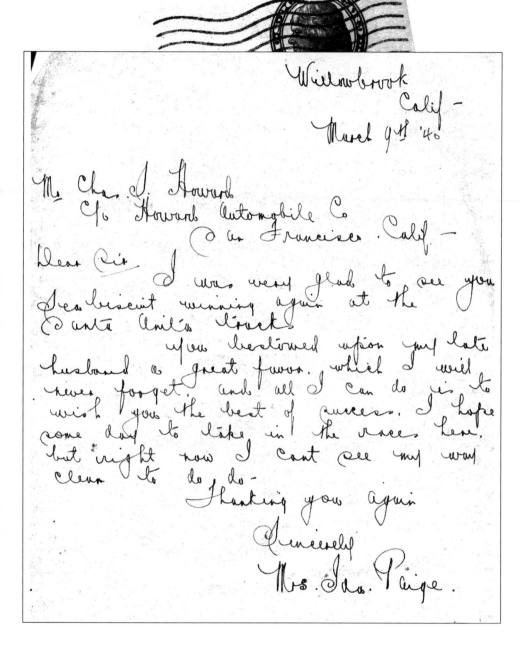

Willowbrook
Calif —
March 9th '40

Mr. Chas. S. Howard
C/o Howard Automobile Co
San Francisco. Calif. —

Dear Sir
                I was very glad to see your
Seabiscuit winning again at the
Santa Anita track
                You bestowed upon my late
husband a great favor, which I will
never forget, and all I can do is to
wish you the best of success. I hope
some day to take in the races here,
but right now I can't see my way
clear to do so —
                Thanking you again
                        Sincerely
                        Mrs. Jas. Paige.

MELVIN CHALONE
ABERDEEN, MARYLAND

March 11, 1940

Mr. Charles S. Howard
1601 Van Ness Ave. at California St.
San Francisco, California

My dear Mr. Howard,

    To you my sincerest congratulations are handed out
for the long awaited acheivement that dear old Seabiscuit
accomplished after three attempts.

    Please pardon these delayed congratulations that
I hold so firm and loyal to a thoroughbred so true and
staunch as Seabiscuit. My hat is off in reverence to
this thoroughbred always, why shouldn't it be?

    I have followed this thoroughbred up over since
he parted company with Wheatley Stables and into better
hands he could not have entered, to a man like you, Mr.
Howard, a perfect gentleman to the utmost, a great sportsman in every respect and the owner of the finest and greatest thoroughbred that ever carried a saddle-Seabiscuit.

    I surely was glad to read this morning that your
thoroughbred and Kentucky Derby elegible Mioland won the
$10,000 San Juan Capistrano handicap at Santa Anita (more
luck to you to win the Kentucky Derby)

    I hope that you accept my congratulations as I feel
toward Seabiscuit. Might I also add that I wish you the
best of luck possible toward owning many more race horses
just like dear old Seabiscuit.

    Wishing you best of luck and sincere wishes, I remain,

                              Sincerely Yours,

                              Melvin Chalone

Indianapolis Ind
March 11 1940

To Mr Charles S. Howard.
Ridgewood Ranch,
Willits California.

Dear Sir;
This morning paper states that you are
retireing your Famous Seabiscuit, and I wish to tell
you, I think that is a very beautiful guesture, and
what he surely deserves.

Seabiscuit is one of the finest Horses that ever
came down the strech. I have never had the honor
of seeing him run, but I have followed him and
bet Him ever since he was a 3 year old, and if
you will believe me, he is my Favorite Horse.

I am a disabled World War Vet, wounded and
shell shocked and this old Vet kneeld down the night
before Seabiscuit last Race and prayed to God that
He would win and my prayer was answered. That
will probably make you laugh, to think a broken down
old Soldier, think His prayer had anything to do with
Seabiscuit winning that Race. I would so much like
a picture of the Champ, but I guess that is asking to
much of you, I would treasure it. I dont get out much
and circumstance wont permit me to buy one. I want
to thank you Mr Howard and please forgive me for
takeing up your valuable time.

Resp Yours
Sgt Leon L. Hayes.
26 So. Capitol Ave.
Indianapolis.
Indiana.

Mar. 11, 1940

Dear Mr. Howard:—

There are some sports writers & others who did not like it for Seabiscuit to defeat War Admiral — & they don't like you or Seabiscuit. And now, they are writing you ~~numerous~~ letters urging you to retire Seabiscuit. They hope his record may be broken. Hope you will continue to race him this year.

a Friend

LOS ANGELES ATHLETIC CLUB

3/12/40

Dear friend Charlie –

I want to congratulate you on your decision to retire the 'Biscuit – It has surely made a hit with the public down here & the hand they gave you last Saturday was genuine & to my mind one of the finest moments I have ever witnessed in the field of Sports.

Personally, while I'm thru betting on horses, you are certainly a splendid "stand out" & the biggest credit to the turf today –

Kindest regards,

Claude Peters –

MANCHESTER BY THE SEA
MASSACHUSETTS

Mar 1ᵗ '40

Dear Mr. Howard,

Todays Post brought us word of your decision to retire the great Seabiscuit. In this I am sure you have the respect of the entire nation.

While we all would give a great deal to see that gallant little fellow again and cheer him on as he'd make his brilliant drive in the home stretch, yet deep in our hearts we realize the many dangers that accompany shipping + racing, so, now, that Our "Sweetheart of the American Turf" is retired in all his glory and fitness, ~~it is a real joy~~ we join in saying — Well Done, Seabiscuit you have earned your crown —

and a will deserved rest, which
you are sure to get from an owner
that has proved more than once
his great faith and love for you.
Sea biscuit will live forever
in our hearts + memories.
He has been an inspiration.

Sincerely,

Ellen S. Henry.

Manchester
Mass,

S. Farrar
122 University Towers Bld.
Montreal, Canada.

March I2 -40

Mr. C.S.Howard

Dear Mr. Howard

Ever since the "Biscuit" was a three year old, he has been
my favorite, and I don't mind telling you I made a few dollars
on him in that period.
I even bet a weeks pay on him the time he ran War Admiral into
the ground, much against the advise of my associates.
Got six to two for my investment too which was just like taking
candy from a kid.
I am glad you decided to retire him as he deserves everything
that can be done for a horse.
Of course you must know that there is a purpose behind this seem-
ingly"fan mail" note to old "Biscuit",and there is too,although
I don't want you to think this is a habit of mine.
Now that we will not see him any more I would very much like to
get a full length picture of him to remember him by,one that I
could frame,and if you have one kicking around that you could spare
I would be very greatfull to receive it.(Postage enclosed)
Hoping you will be able to oblige me at this time,

I remain,

Yours truly.

Farrar

Auntie Mar's generosity was legendary, if you admired her hat, she'd give it to you!

S. F. Mar. 12, 1940.

Dear Mr. Howard; So
glad that dear "Sea-
biscuit" is to have
a Vacation on your
ranch. Such a darling
horse. How I prayed
that he would win.
I knew he would.
Please see that no one
steals or hurts him
on the ranch.
Best wishes for "Seabiscuit"
and all your fine
horses.

Respectfully,
an admirer of
"Seabiscuit"

Mr. C. R. Howard,
Howard Auto. Co.,
San Francisco,
Calif.

ROBERT MEYER HOTELS

*HOTEL EMERSON
BALTIMORE, MD.

HOTEL STACY-TRENT
TRENTON, N. J.

*HOTEL PATRICK HENRY†
ROANOKE, VA.

WINDSOR HOTEL†
JACKSONVILLE, FLA.

*HOTEL ROOSEVELT
JACKSONVILLE, FLA.

*THE HERMITAGE
NASHVILLE, TENN.

*HOTEL FARRAGUT†
KNOXVILLE, TENN.

*HOTEL WINECOFF
ATLANTA, GA.

*HOTEL SIR WALTER†
RALEIGH, N.C.

*RADIO IN EVERY ROOM
DIRECT CONNECTED GARAGE†

HOTEL SIR WALTER

"RALEIGH'S LARGEST AND FINEST HOTEL"

RULAND A. MUMFORD, MANAGER

RALEIGH, N.C.

march 12

Dear Seabiscuit,

I am glad you won the
Santa Anita and are famous
like I. There you have been
retired, I have been retired
19 or 30 years I can't ~~remember~~
remember. When you come
to the beautiful bluegrass country of Lexington Ky (I stay at
Samuel Riddles Far Away
Farms) look me up.

EVERY ROOM AN OUTSIDE ROOM, WITH RADIO AND CIRCULATING ICE WATER
CEILING FANS

I would like you to write me a letter about your life, don't forget to sent it to me.

I had Joe my stable boy paste your picture on the salt brick so I could lick you every day. It made me seem closer to you.

I am glad you beat Kayak II and I didn't agree with Henry Mc Lemore when he said Kayak could have beat you if he had a chance.

Your friend,
Man O'War
alias
Teresa Wohl
128 Groveland Ave.
Raleigh, N. C.

PENNSYLVANIA 6-5300

ADOLPHE PONS
II WEST 42ND STREET
ROOM 400
NEW YORK, N. Y.

March 14th, 1940

Mr. Charles S. Howard,
San Francisco, California

My dear Mr. Howard:-

      I want to congratulate you on your decision of retiring your marvellous horse SEABISCUIT, and I know he is destined to become one of the great stallions of America.

      Of course, I am deeply interested in the welfare of both of your wonderful horses SEABISCUIT and KAYAK II. They are from bloodlines nearest my heart, and I have an honest affection for all the FAIR PLAY and ROCK SAND BLOOD. I was associated with the late August Belmont for twenty seven years, and had charge of matings and breeding of his famous mares. In fact I recommended the purchase in England of TOPIARY, the dam of TRACERY, also FAIRY GOLD, the dam of FAIR PLAY, and both your horses are direct descendants of these great sires. This line is so strong that it is bound to continue.

      KAYAK II should suit the Fair Play blood admirably, and both horses' best matings would be through Domino, Teddy, Ben Brush, Sunstar and Spearmint.

      Wishing you great luck in your breeding enterprise, and with kindest regards, to you and Mrs. Howard.

             Sincerely yours,

             Adolphe Pons

V. GONZALEZ GRAU
MANUFACTURERS REPRESENTATIVE
P. O. BOX 2992 2408
SAN JUAN, PUERTO RICO

March 14, 1941

Mr. Charles S. Howard,
Los Angeles, Calif.

Dear Mr. Howard:-

   For several years I have been following up the magnificent
demonstrations with which your horses have been consecrating your
name in the turf history of the World. It is worthy of praise
the contribution that your stable has made to the Kind of Sports,
not only in the continental U. S. but all over the World, insuf-
flating enthusiasm to all sympathizers and raising the standars
of this sport to the highest level since the times of Man O'War.

   Your name and that of Seabiscuit (EL BIZCOCHO, as we call him
in Spanish), will long endure in the annals of horse-racing history;
not only for the reason of being the greatest money winner of all
times, but for the interesting story of his life and the brave dignity
of his achievements. He is not an ordinary horse; he was born with
the soul of Pegasus or Rocinante.

   I am a very enthusiastic horse-racing sympathizer and still a
better admirer of the Biscuit (consequently, you too) and I keep
an album of all pictures I have been able to obtain of Seabiscuit.
I have one here he is posing besides his statue at Santa Anita, with
you holding him. I have another of his seven sons and daughters,
all of which look marvelously. Also another here you are pictured
riding your white pony.

   Honestly, Ie would be delighted if some day I could visit your
stable and see the Biscuit personally. But is a very long way from
Puerto Rico to California.

   I sincerely trust that you are as democratic as you look in
pictures and will not deny to me the privilege of receiving a few
lines in answer.

   With best regard, I remain

                                    Cordially yours,

vgg/nl   V. Gonzalez Grau

87

CHARLES A. ROSSIER
417 MONTGOMERY STREET
SAN FRANCISCO, CALIFORNIA

March 14th, 1940.

Dear Mr. Howard:--

      I lost my beloved wife a month ago after a lingering illness covering a period of two years. During this time she retained her cheerfulness and courage to the end. Mercifully she at no time suffered pain.

      During it all she followed the fortunes of Seabiscuit and never once lost her faith in his stout heart.

      I framed the letter to you she so hopefully signed, which brought from you that heart-warming response and your splendid gift of the last of Seabiscuit's shoes when he won over War Admiral at Pimlico in that never to be forgotten World Classic, which she listened to over the radio.

      This is a quotation from one of her close friends who was with her when she passed away:

> "Wouldn't little Lotta have had a thrill over the race with Seabiscuit coming home with new honors and Kayak a close second! Let's hope she could see and enjoy it! I have never known her to prize anything so dearly as she did the shoe of Seabiscuit and the letter from the owner, Mr. Howard. So wonderful it came when it did to give her all that joy when she needed it so badly".

      What a pity she could not have listened in on this his crowning victory at Santa Anita. I like to think she did - and perhaps saw it.

      I know she would want me to send you my warmest congratulations for your long-waited-for victory, which I now most heartily do.

      She had planned to motor to Mendocino County this summer to once again pay her respects to her Beloved favorite and to Fair Knightess too, whom she so admired when she last saw her at Tanforan.

      I wish for you continued success with Kayak II and send you my most fervent hopes for Mioland at Churchill Downs in May.

Very Sincerely Yours,

To:
Mr. Charles S. Howard,
1601 Van Ness Ave., City.

CHARLES A. ROSSIER
417 MONTGOMERY STREET
SAN FRANCISCO. CALIFORNIA

March 28th, 1940.

Mr. Charles S. Howard,
1601 Van Ness Avenue,
San Francisco, California.

Dear Mr. Howard:--

Yours March 18th from Pasadena:-

It was nice of you to take the
time to write to me in between all the activities of
your peripatetic movements, and I appreciate your kind
expressions of sympathy.

I accept with pleasure your kind
invitation to stop in and visit your ranch near Willits
and to pay my respects to the 'Biscuit should I be
motoring through Mendocino County this coming Summer.
It would give me much pleasure to avail myself of this
privilege.   Mrs. Rossier would love to have me do
this I feel sure.

Sincerely yours,

CAR/el

Magnolia Tex.
3-15-40

Dear Sir

Reading of Gallant Little Seabiscuit becoming King, after all the brave struggles he has made, inspired me to try to express my regards of him with paint brush and pen & ink, in Picture and Poem. I am no artist or poetess either. I am merely a farm wife and mother of eleven children, all alive & average normal youngsters. 9 are at home all school age or under. We are poor, but not on relief though some times we do not know where the next day groceries are to come from. but they allways come and _____ our own honest efforts. _____ truly hope you are pleased with this picture and verse. I am _____ like you, Seabiscuit has well earned his retirement and I admire _____ consideration. we had an _____ horse, and in his youth he was the fastest thing on these Prairies, but he got a leg broke hurt when he was about 20 years old & we put him in a swing & splinted his leg. it healed kinda crooked, but he still could out run the "Pound mens nags" when he died at 36 years of age. he would get out and those pound men would spot him and take after him & 9 would see him coming, throwing that game leg, & 9 would open the gate & he would run inside & then turn around and grin at the angry pound men. we called him "Peeler". most Respectfully 9 am

mrs. Clara Gay Sager   P.S. "Peeler" was racing strain.
R. 1. magnolia Texas   he was dark red, black long tail &

"SEABISCUIT, THE KING."

"NOBLE SEABISCUIT, SO GALLANT, BRAVE AND TRUE
    THE HORSE RACING WORLD PAYS, TRUE HOMAGE TO YOU
AND ALL THE NEWSPAPERS, YOUR LOUD PRAISES SING
    FOR YOU ARE THE UNDISPUTED, RACE HORSE KING."

"YOU HAVE HAD A HARD LIFE, BUT THOSE DAYS ARE OVER
    THE REST OF YOUR DAYS, WILL BE SPENT IN THE CLOVER
ONLY SEVEN YEARS OLD, BAY BOY, AND THE KING
    OH GALLANT SEABISCUIT, YOU VICTORY BELLS RING."

"MY VALIANT HORSEFRIEND, THIS WAS YOUR LAST RACE
    NOW I AM TAKING YOU, TO A BEAUTIFULL PLACE
FOR YOU WON THE SANTA ANITA HANDICAP BY SPEED
    AND NOW YOU ARE KING, YOU CAME IN, IN THE LEAD."

"YOU CAME UP FROM THE RANKS, MY COURAGEOUS FRIEND
    BUT YOUR DAYS OF STRUGGLE, ARE NOW AT AN END
YOU ARE NOW RETIRED, AND I AM TAKING YOU HOME
    MY DEAR LITTLE BAY, YOU ARE KING ON YOUR THRONE."

Metro-Goldwyn-Mayer Studio
Culver City, California

Mervyn LeRoy

                                        March 15th
                                        1 9 4 0

        Dear Charlie:

        Cannot tell you how much I appreciate
        your 'phone call. Also want to thank
        you for giving me one of the first
        services on SEABISCUIT. Please let
        me know three or four weeks ahead so
        I can ease her down for it.

        Hope you have many SEABISCUITS and
        that even I get half a cracker some
        day.

                        Sincerely,

                        [signature: Merv]

        Mr. C. S. Howard
        Huntington Hotel
        Pasadena, Calif.

        ml.h

March 20, 1940

Mr. Chas. S. Howard,

Dear Sir:

I do not approve of your retirement of Seabiscuit, and I am only one of many. I think that he should have been brought East to parade at each track, and not be sent into oblivion just because he won the race at Santa Ani ta. He is too good to send into retirement so soon. Sun Beau raced until he was nine years old. There is really no opposition for Seabiscuit here in the East, so you would not have to worry about the likelihood of his being defeated in any race. He should meet Challedon. He has carried 133 lbs., and the weight did not keep him from winning. I think he could beat Challedon May 8, but I do not think Kayakll can do so with 134 lbs on him. Besides no one cares anything about the latter. He is not a popular figure as is Seabiscuit. I think you should bring Seabiscuit East, and run him in one more race at each track this season in a glorious farewell appearance. You horsemen are always so anxious to retire your horses to stud that you do not give them the chance to really become immortal figures on the turf. I still hope you will bring Seabiscuit back for this season, and wait until next winter to retire him permanently. He needs it to make him the greatest of them all, instead of merely one of the great horses. Reconsider, and let's see Seabiscuit the first $500,000 winner, and the greatest of them all for all time.

A fan.

C.H.D. File No.

UNITED STATES FLEET
HAWAIIAN DETACHMENT   **EA/vo**

U.S.S. INDIANAPOLIS, Flagship,
c/o Fleet Post Office,
Pearl Harbor, T. H.,
21 March, 1940.

Mr. Charles S. Howard,
San Francisco, Calif.

Dear Mr. Howard:

This letter is written in behalf of the
Chief Petty Officers Mess of the USS INDIANAPOLIS.

When your much admired horse, Seabiscuit,
romped home the winner in the big Santa Anita handi-
cap all hands had that happy sparkle in their eyes
and felt mighty good about it. It was a very great
accomplishment for Seabiscuit; we feel almost as
proud of him as you do. It is with much regret
that we heard the news of his retirement, but he
has proven himself the Champ of all Champions and
now deserves the quiet and peaceful life that belongs
to him.

As so many of the fellows in this Mess
are more or less 'dyed-in-the-wool' horse fans, we
are asking you to send our Mess a colored photograph
(with your autograph), or a pair of his shoes or
some other appropriate souvenir that will be perman-
ently displayed in the Chief Petty Officers quarters.
We will be more than glad to defray any expense in-
volved for cost of souvenir, shipping, etc.

Trusting very sincerely that I may hear
from you in the near future, and hoping that you
will be kind enough to send us something that we can
proudly have displayed in our Mess, I am,

Very truly yours,

Evert Anderson.

E. ANDERSON,
Chief Watertender,
United States Navy.

Sent pictures

The U.S.S. Indianapolis was torpedoed and sank July 30, 1945

MEMBERS
JOHN LAWLER, Lake Preston
STANLEY BARNETT, Winner
FRED L. VILAS, Pierre
CHAIRMAN

South Dakota Racing Commission

Lake Preston ~~Winner~~ S. D. 3 - 26 - 40.

Seabiscuit,

    San Frahsisco, Cal:-

Dear Old Seabiscuit :-

    Here is to you and to you again may your shadow never grow less.
And I have often thought how lucky you was when you fell into the hands of
Mr. Smith as trainer and Mr. Howard as owner both had confidence in your ability
and knew that all you needed was a little help from the goddess of luck and you
would go to the top and you have proven to them and the world that their faith
was well founded and dont overlook the boy that sat up there in the pilot house
in so many of your winning races Red Pollard and with those old legs bothering
you several times in your racing days you must have had a pretty good Vet. around
and last but not least is the boy that looked after your ever want and when the
owner trainer jockey Vet was pounding their ear he was still in your stall look-
after those old feavered legs and many a good horse has gone to the scrap heap
just for the want of a good care taker.
Now Seabiscuit I am glad to here that you are to be retired and I no that you
will be running in a nice big paddock with plenty of green grass and nice cool
water for the rest of ypur days what a contrast to some of the old timers that
we see out to the bush tracks. And there is one more thing I would like to have
you do have one of your sons come on and win the Kentucky Derby and you will
have that chance with Mr. Howard behind you I am an old time horseman but was
always with the harness horses. I had a slight stroke and my ald age does not
look as bright as yours does Seabiscuit but I know you will miss that bugle call
as much as I will miss the good friends I have around the tracks. So I will close
this letter with best wishes for your success in the stud.

           One of your thousands of admires

                      J. W. LAWLER.

J. W. LAWLER
LAKE PRESTON. S. DAK.

LAKE PRESTON
MAR 27
16 -PM
1940
S. DAK.

Seabiscuit,

    San Francisco,

        Cal.

Chas Howard Auto Co.

Mr. C H Howard
Los Angeles
Calif.

1439 7th Church St
Decatur Ill
March 24-4[?]

Dear Sir, your wonderful
gift was recieved by me.
The Record your horse
has made is wonderful
Credit to all involved
Mr Smith, Pollard, Woolf,
and Your self. I firmly believe
if Pollard had ridden the horse
he wouldn't have been Second
in previous Races. Some horses
are partial to team work Like Pollard's
and Woolf is a Good Second.
        Best Wishes for The Stable
                            Elmer Bogle

P.S. I am not a nut but your horse is wonderful.

Here in This Stall it is
Conceeded by all, a horse
Whose Record will Never fall.
May his Years Be Long.
As a Sire to be
And his offSprings Like
The Biscuit Be.
Cool, headed, Sinceer Ready
to him. Not Be in the
Race. As a fill out for fun.

CD.

PASADENA, CALIF
MAR 26-1940

MR.AND MRS.C.S.HOWARD,
HUNTINGTON,HOTEL
PASADENA,CALIFORNIA.

DEAR MR.AND MRS.HOWARD:

HAVING FOR MANY WEEKS NOW BEEN ONE OF THE MOST ARDENT ADMIRERS AND
BOOSTERS OF THE GREAT ''SEABISCUIT''IT DOES NOT SEEM TOO FAR OUT OF
ORDER THAT I SHOULD BE THE ONE TO WIN THE SEABISCUIT TROPHY FOR BEST
COCKER SPANIEL THAT YOU SO GENEROUSLY OFFERS TO THE WEST COAST COCKER
SPANIEL CLUB THIS YEAR.

WHILE WE FEEL THAT WE HAVE A GREAT DOG AND THAT HE HAS WON A LOT OF
HONORS HERETOFORE NOTHING HAS BEEN SO WONDERFUL AS THIS AND IT IS BY
FAR AND AWAY THE MOST HANDSOME TROPHY WE HAVE EVER WON.

OUR SINCEREST THANKS TO YOU AND OUR BEST WISHES FOR THE CONTINUANCE OF
THE GREAT SUCCESS OF THE HOWARD STABLES.

MARY JANE VILSACK AND W.HOYT CATER
GAMING ACRES COCKER SPANIELS,

W. Hoyt Cater

915 S. Carondelet St. Los. Angeles.
April 1st 1943

Mr C. S. Howard.

Dear Mr. Howard.

You will never know how happy. I was today. when I received the beautiful autographed Photograph. of your magnificent. horse. Seabiscuit. and his. brave little Jockey.

I wept. for Joy on that. memorable day when he swept into Victory. And to think. that. you his owner would "take time" to do a kindness like that. From the bottom of my heart. I thank you. I shall get it framed. and "Seabiscuit." will be among my most. treasured possessions. and may you realize greater success. with your splendid animal in the reproductive field, and may he transmit to his "Children" the splendid qualities. with which nature has so bountifully bestowed upon him.

I am not. Miss Coburn but. Mrs Coburn. a grand mother sixty four years old. I was

born, and raised, on a
Canadian farm, and I know
and love horses, I have
revised the poem and I
think it is much prettier.
and I am inclosing two copies.
I hope you will tack one up
in Sea biscuits stable.
How I would love to caress his
silky nose, how beautiful he
is, lovely head, ears, and neck,
wonderful chest muscles and
graceful body, one of natures
masterpieces. again I wish to
thank you. gratefully yours

(Mrs) Ida Ruth Coburn.
9158 Carondelet. St—
Los. Angeles. Calif...

Seabiscuit:
They say. You are only a horse,
That you have no soul.
Ah . but you fell and rose again;.
You won the goal.
Not for the gold thats showered down
Nor for the fame that wins a crown.
But because you are brave, and strong, and true.
You led the way for others to do.
You never stopped to be moan your fate;
But turned again. to the "starting gate"
With head erect, and nostrils. wide.
You took the turf "with a mighty stride,
all honor to those who run again.
From the ranks of weary, beaten, men,
When your foot-ships flag. on life's weary way.
Remember Seabiscuit who won today.

                                    Ida Ruth Coburn
                                    april 1940.

=1= West Los Angeles Cal
April 1, 1940.

Dear Papa SeaBiscuit,
Why are they trying to take the name Biscuit away from "your Family", and why should they?

Would "you" mind me suggesting as an Honor to "your many thousand fans, and admirers, the Name, Our Biscuit, for the first Boy. And Don't you think, the name. Biscuit should remain in the family such as. Good. Biscuit, Brown. Biscuit. Golden. Biscuit. Hot Biscuit, Light Biscuit, And in case of Daughters. Dottie Biscuit's, and winnie Biscuit. I feel we would have more to remember you by.

Don't "you think? it would be nice, for, when "your public is at the track, for them to be able to say their goes our Biscuit,

-2-

If I Could converse with.
"You, I sure. I Could tell you. how
the first Boy. could. Pay his way
through school. and also Pay his
Brothers and Sisters, way through.
Well heare hopeing Your.
future Children all the luck ther
is; and as one of "Your many fans.
I hope. for their success.
Yours Truley.
    Kent Johnson.
    11541 Rochester ave
    West Los Angeles.

P.S. Oh." never mind the Cigars
Realey I don't smoke. them.

Warner Bros. Pictures. Inc.

WEST COAST STUDIOS

BURBANK, CALIF.

OFFICE OF PRESIDENT

April 1, 1940

Mr. C. S. Howard
Howard Automobile Agency
1601 Van Ness Avenue
San Francisco, California

My dear Howard:

Thanks for your letter of the 27th and I hope you don't forget to pick up SHANGAY LILY when you take LADY MARSCO to your ranch. I am now arranging my next year's breeding and I am figuring on two mares for SEABISCUIT as I do want to keep related to you, as you are not only a good horseman but a lucky fellow.

I have some mares who have already been bred this year that I may want to use for this purpose. One is BRIDGEEN who is the dam of THE FIGHTER by BULL DOG. I now have two colts from her by MAN O'WAR--one two years old and one a yearling. She has also dropped a filly this year bred to TOP ROW, and I re-bred her to TOP ROW. She is an excellent brood-mare and naturally want to keep her with good strains.

Hoping that LADY MARSCO and SHANGAY LILY will drops colts that SEABISCUIT will be proud of, which naturally makes you proud, I am, with kindest regards,

Sincerely,

H. M. Warner

HMW:sl

Dayton - Ohio
april 3, 1940

Dear Mr. Howard,

I want to thank you so much for the picture of Seabiscuit. It was grand of you to send it to me with your autograph on it. This autographed picture will go in my scrapbook with the rest of the "biscuit's" pictures and articles.

I hope someday to come out to California and see Seabiscuit and the rest of California.

Thank you again for the picture.

Yours truly,

Ann Bancroft

BETTING SYSTEM

by

BILL FISHER

The races were on, and low with remorse

The boys were all trying to pick a good horse.

There were four of us there who thought we knew ponies,

But when bets were placed they always were phonies.

Each had his turn at blasting derision

And now gazed in his glass blindly hoping for vision,

When all of a sudden there was somebody hollared,

"I see a big horse well ridden by Pollard."

Another one yelled, "It must be Seabiscuit."

I said, "Come on boys, supposing we risk it."

Oh, then we all knew it was not a myth,

For there in the paddock was silent Tom Smith.

I will not say each was in his cup

But I know I heard the Biscuit speak up.

He boastin ly said, "I am not a coward,

I'll win this big race for good Charlie Howard."

He pranced to the gate while all the crowd roared,

We hastened to bet across the tote board.

Seabiscuit and Kayak won first place and second,

And this was the time we rightly had reckoned.

Now Pollard and Seabiscuit both are retired

And we four are waiting for ponies he sired.

Dear Mr. Howard.
please name stabscuits
Colt Hot Biscuit
I told you up at your
ranch, a little friend

Nancy Harp
605. Clay St
Ukiah. Cal.

Mr. Howard: My second graders wrote these stories about Sea Biscuit. I thought they were funny. Dispose of them after you read them.

Mildred Schwarz

San Juan Capistrano

Marjorie

Sea biscuit was in the barn. He was in a race. I saw his picture. He won the race. They put a wreath around his head. He got a blue ribbon. His master was happe.

Yeko

Seabiscuit was in the barn. He is going to have a race. Seabiscuit was a good horse. Seabiscuit won the race. Seabiscuit got a blue ribbon.

Ruby.

Seabiscuit was in the barn.
He had a race.
He won the race.
He got a blue ribbon.
I saw a picture of him in the paper. He was raceing when I saw him in the paper.

Patsy.

Seabiscuit was in the barn
He Was in a race. He won
the race. Seabiscuit got a
blue ribbon. Seabiscuit was
very happy. Thay put flowe
o all over him.

Paul Richard

Sea biscuit was in the barn. He
He lived in a big barn Yard. He has
pleanty to eat. He is healthy. He was
in a race. He won the race. They put
a red and blue wreath around
the hores.

Tulsa, Okla.
1315 E 26 st

JCS

Dear Mr. Howard:

I am one of the great army of the horse lovers of america. I am a great admirer of your two most famous horses, Kayak II and Seabiscut. Although I am but a boy of twelve I love horses as I know you most love them If it is not asking to much would you send me a picture of Kayak and Seabiscut.

a fellow Horse Lover
Jim Curd
Tulsa, Oklahoma
1315 E. 26 st

1402 South First Ave
Phoenix, Arizona

Dear Mr. Howard;

I am a mexican boy, fifteen years old, living in Phoenix and have made it my hobby to collect autographes of famous people.

I have been formutate in the past in acquiring a large number of Celebrities autographes here in Phoenix and would sincerely appreciate yours.

I am enclosing card for your signature.

Thanks in advance,
Very Truly Yours,
Ruben Limas.

P.S. I would like to have your signature so I could display it at the Phx Hobby Show here in Phoenix next week.
Thanks — Pal.

1402 South First Ave
Phoenix, Arizona

Charles S. Howard
Ranch
c/o Charles S. Howard
Willits,
California

"out west"

338 Lexington Avenue
New York, N.Y.

Dear Mr. Howard:

Like the millions of other Seabiscuit admirers I was
glad to see he is being retired in a blazy of glory.

My heart was broken, twice, at Santa Anita when he was
robbed of first place in the handicap.

When I came East - to hear nothing but War Admiral -
I fought the Biscuit's battles from one end of Manhattan to the
other. When he ran his great race in Maryland I was as proud as
though I was Swing On.

And when he achieved your ambition (and mine), to become
the greatest money-winner of all time you'd have thought it was
my money he was winning - even though I didn't have a penny riding
on his lovely nose.

And so, loving him, and admiring him, I'm glad to know
he will rest and grow fat and happy and leave the track undisputed
hero of all time.

You own the greatest horse in the world today - at
least you THINK you own him - actually he is the property of all
of us who love thoroughbreds - and recognize that a horse has
something else besides the ability to earn a few dollars for the
gambling public.

And so, Mr. Howard, I salute Seabiscuit - the greatest
little thoroughbred that ever was saddled - I hope he lives to
a ripe old age - and gives you many colts and fillies - all with
the ability to run, and the great heart of their father.

Sincerely,

Helen T. Thompson

The Town House
WILSHIRE BOULEVARD
LOS ANGELES
EXPOSITION 1234

The Drake
CHICAGO
The Blackstone
CHICAGO
The Evanshire
EVANSTON
The Town House
LOS ANGELES

A. S. KIRKEBY
MANAGING DIRECTOR

Dear Marcella and Charlie, Knowing
that you would have millions of
phone calls and telegrams, decided
to take this means of again congratulating you on your marvelous victory.
I do not blame you for hiding out
to watch the race. I personally felt the
need of the Seil Mac crying room
after the race. Have not fully recovered
yet.
We are leaving for home today. The
excitement is over. Vic joins me in
wishing you continued good luck and
Seabiscuit many petit fours just like
his gallant self.

Sincerely
Rene Klinker

Barbara Howard at the National Museum of Racing and Hall of Fame, Saratoga Springs, New York

ABOUT BARBARA HOWARD

Born in Cheyenne County, Kansas, Mrs. Howard attended Butler University in Indianapolis and graduated from the University of Arizona with a degree in education. For a short time, she was a teacher and rancher in Tucson, Arizona, which was followed by twenty years of racehorse ranching with her husband Lindsay Howard Jr., grandson of C. S. Howard, in the Thousand Oaks area of California.

Mrs. Howard now resides in Monarch Beach, California. The mother of Michael, Lisa, and Malinda Howard, she is also the grandmother of Jessica, Rachel, Meredith, Nathan, and Karen Howard, and Camden Howard Grant. Howard's niece, Marita Biven, named her daughter after Marcela Zabala Howard, the wife of C. S. Howard and proud owner of Seabiscuit.

Mrs. Howard would like people to know that God has been good to her and that one highlight in her life was the eight years she spent in Bible Study Fellowship, which she considers to be a blessing.

Now, the second life of Seabiscuit, provided through the book by Laura Hillenbrand, she is adding a new, fun, and exciting dimension to her life. Thanks go to her son Michael, friend May Brown, and Stan Standefer, for all giving the extra push to do the book.